You are not right, sir!

"The thing about these cars is that they're fail-safe. These cars are made like tanks. They have the best engine and the best transmission, they're totally safe."
—Actor James Dean, about his Porsche Spyder roadster, which failed him only a few weeks later, in a deadly crash

"He has no voice at all—he cannot sing."
—Enrico Caruso's teacher

"I would have never owned those ugly-ass shoes."
—Defendant O.J. Simpson, in his 1996 civil lawsuit deposition, denying he owned a pair of Bruno Magli shoes, as worn by the murderer of Nicole Simpson and Ron Goldman. One month later, thirty photographs were discovered, showing Simpson wearing the same shoes at a 1993 Buffalo Bills game.

From parents who had no faith in their children ("I have an idiot for a son" —sculptor Auguste Rodin's father), to generals who underestimated their enemies ("Why, they couldn't hit an elephant with . . ." —Union General John B. Sedgewick, about a Confederate assault, in a statement he was unable to complete because he was hit by a bullet), this sidesplitting sequel proves once again that two *Wrongs!* don't make a right, but they do make for an hilarious reading experience.

JANE O'BOYLE is a writer who lives in Charleston, South Carolina. Her other books include the first *Wrong!* and *Free Drinks for Ladies with Nuts* (both available from Plume), and *Catnip for the Soul*.

For Mom and Dad

> *"Whenever a man does a thoroughly stupid thing, it is always from the noblest of motives."*
>
> —Oscar Wilde

Nobody's perfect. I suspect that deep in her past, even Martha Stewart has buried a carbonized carrot muffin and a dead orchid. But blunders are nothing to be ashamed of. Mistakes serve to jar you back into reality, and force you to address a situation with a totally new perspective. That is, with hope.

Years ago, when some woman at a tollhouse tried to make chocolate cookies, she flubbed the recipe by not melting the chocolate first. She just cut the chocolate into little chips. (What would Martha have done?) Looking on the bright side of her culinary shortsightedness, this half-baked baker pronounced the creations "chocolate chip" cookies instead. The world has never been the same.

The person who doesn't make mistakes is someone who doesn't make anything. This book is an all-new collection of "famous last words" and erroneous predictions, to inspire readers to eventual glory when they've just committed a colossal embarrassment. This does not give you an excuse to break the law or to hurt another living being. But you do have the freedom to look or sound like an idiot and not feel guilty about it anymore. This is the principle on which our country was founded, after all. Blunder large or small, and you will be in diverse and perhaps surprising company. This book contains goofs from Thomas Edison and Prince Philip to Barbara Walters and Al Gore.

Truly wise people know that in the end, they won't regret their mistakes. People who are annoyingly flawless, who possess cartloads of common sense—they are the ones who regret the things they might have achieved, if only they'd screwed up once or twice.

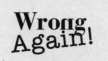

Wrong Again!

Arts and Literature

Some people do not have a knack for recognizing the potential in an artist. And many artists have a tendency to err. Fortunately for us, they kept on trying.

"Hopeless as a composer."

—Beethoven's music teacher, who thought his student handled the violin very poorly

❧

"Thou shalt commit adultery."

—The seventh commandment, as it appeared in a Bible printed in London in 1631. The printers were fined 3,000 pounds by local authorities, but probably the offenders thought it was worth every penny.

> **"He has no talent at all. . . . Tell him please to give up painting."**

—Painter Edouard Manet to Claude Monet in 1864, regarding a young new artist named Pierre Auguste Renoir

↬

In the novel *Don Quixote*, writer Miguel de Cervantes made several continuity errors. For example, Sancho Panza sells his donkey, but a little while later, he is riding it again. He loses his wallet, which also reappears later in the story without explanation. He then loses his food and destroys his helmet, but somehow, these things reappear when he needs them later.

It is details like these that make English Lit. class very challenging for certain students.

↬

> **"I have an idiot for a son."**

—The father of sculptor Auguste Rodin, who was rejected for admission to art school three times

↬

> "The journalistic scoop of the post–World War II period."

—Editors at the German magazine *Stern* in 1983, when it acquired what editors thought were 63 volumes of Adolf Hitler's diaries "pulled from the wreckage of a cargo plane nine days before Hitler's death in 1945." Two British historians proclaimed the diaries genuine, even though handwriting experts said it was not Hitler's handwriting. Then, some of the pristine book binding was found to contain polyester thread, which was invented long after World War II. *Stern* was considered the journalistic dupe of the post–World War II period.

❧

On August 26, 1989, *TV Guide* put Oprah Winfrey on its cover, showing readers a sexy sleek body. The body turned out to belong to Ann-Margret, in a photo swiped from a previous *TV Guide* cover.

❧

In 1971, McGraw-Hill and Time-Life paid Clifford Irving $1 million for his "autobiography" of Howard Hughes. Hughes was still alive and knew nothing about such a book, but Irving gambled that the eccentric billionaire was such a recluse he would not bother to publicly disclaim the book. Hughes may have had a Spruce Goose, but he didn't have that many screws loose. Irving spent seventeen months in prison.

3

"They were slippers of glass."

—The English version of "Cinderella," originally translated from the French by Charles Perrault, contained an error that was never fixed. Perrault translated *pantouffles en verre* (glass slippers) instead of *pantouffles en vair* (squirrel fur slippers). This may explain why fuzzy slippers never took off as evening wear.

⸎

"AUTOBIOGRAPHY SKEWERS KANSAS SEN. BOB DOLE"

—Headline in *The Boulder Daily Camera*

Memorable Moments from Hollywood

The entertainment industry is a veritable font of inspirational blunders.

"You'll rue the day."

—Leading man Emil Jannings to *The Blue Angel* director Josef von Sternberg in 1929, chastising him for selecting Marlene Dietrich, whom he regarded as unremarkable and untalented, to co-star in the movie. Jannings remained so perturbed that, in one scene where his character strangles hers, he was indeed strangling Dietrich, and her terror is quite real. Sternberg never rued the day he cast Dietrich, however, as the film became the vehicle to stardom for both.

❧

"And I'll sue you for using the word Brothers!"

—Groucho Marx in 1946 to Warner Bros., who threatened to sue Marx for calling a film "A Night in Casablanca" when they had their own film called "Casablanca."

"It won't work with Joan Crawford."

—*Mildred Pierce* movie director Michael Curtiz to producers in 1945, despairing that Bette Davis and Barbara Stanwyck had turned down the title role. Crawford won an Academy Award for *Mildred Pierce*.

❧

"It'll never amount to anything."

—Actor Buddy Ebsen in 1942, about the new medium of television. After *Davy Crockett, The Beverly Hillbillies,* and *Barnaby Jones*, television amounted to the bulk of Ebsen's career.

❧

"[Television] won't be able to hold on to any market it captures after the first six months. People will soon get tired of staring at a plywood box every night."

—Darryl F. Zanuck, head of 20 Century-Fox Studios, 1946

❧

"The thing about these cars is that they're fail-safe. These cars are made like tanks. They have the best engine and the best transmission, they're totally safe."

—Actor James Dean in 1955 about his Porsche Spyder roadster, which failed him only a few weeks later, in a deadly crash

❧

"Unfunny, silly, and totally boring."

—A Philip Morris executive in 1955 who recommended his company not sponsor a new TV show called *I Love Lucy*

❧

"That babe's way too young and pretty to play a middle-aged Irish housewife. Now quit wasting my time."

—Jackie Gleason to his television producers in 1955, rejecting the audition of Audrey Meadows for his new TV show, *The Honeymooners*. Crafty Meadows went home and took off her make-up, put on shabby clothes, and fried some eggs, getting a photographer to capture her "looking awful." When Gleason saw the photos, he gave the role of Alice Kramden to Meadows, who made it one of the most memorable in television history.

"Joe, you've never heard such cheering!"

—Marilyn Monroe to her husband, after making a trip to Korea to entertain American troops. Her husband at the time was Joe DiMaggio.

∽

"It's a dirty picture."

—Actor James Stewart's elderly father, who disapproved of his son's 1959 appearance in *Anatomy of a Murder*, the first movie to deal frankly with the topic of rape. The aging Stewart took out print ads in his hometown paper, advising the public not to see this film. Mayor Richard Daley banned *Anatomy of a Murder* from the city of Chicago, because the courtroom dialogue contained such words as "intercourse" and "contraceptive." The film was nominated for seven Academy Awards, including Best Picture.

∽

"Too disturbing for Kansasans."

—The state of Kansas in 1959, when it banned Billy Wilder's movie *Some Like It Hot* from playing in theaters throughout the state. It was banned not because of the cross-dressing characters but because of Tony Curtis's steamy love scenes with Marilyn Monroe.

"Stiff, unappealing . . . not a good actor. You ain't got it, kid. You ain't got it! Get the f——out of my office."

—Columbia producer Jerry Tokovsky to an aspiring actor named Harrison Ford, in 1965

❦

"Sorry, we're not casting any young men today."

—TV executive in 1962 who heard actress Suzanne Pleshette's voice without looking up

❦

"I will say this about McGavin. He is going to be a very disappointed man on the first Easter after his death."

—Burt Reynolds in 1963, about his *Riverboat* TV show co-star and personal nemesis, Darren McGavin. Reynolds was familiar with disappointment, as his role was written out of the TV series in the middle of its first season.

❦

> "If this series goes five years, I will be only thirty-three and rich. Then I can stop and do something I'd enjoy more. I want to be a schoolteacher. That would be a real challenge."

—Bill Cosby, star of *I Spy*, in 1965. It was an even greater challenge than he suspected, as he never achieved his goal.

❧

> "I'll be right back."

—Actor Warren Beatty, at dinner with his girlfriend, Natalie Wood, excused himself from their table at Chasen's. He never returned. When he went to Wood's home a week later to pick up his clothes, he learned that they had been burned.

❧

> "Any show with a frog as the host won't work."

—CBS executives, turning down the pilot for Jim Henson's *The Muppet Show* in the early 1970s. No one thought these *Sesame Street*–style characters would appeal to adults. Rejected by all the networks, Henson resorted to production in England, and the show was then syndicated in the U.S. *The Muppet Show* was soon viewed in 100 countries, by 235 million people, and became the inspiration for several feature films.

While signing his autograph in cement along the Hollywood Walk of Fame, actor Burt Reynolds misspelled his name.

❧

Producers' first choice to play television's *Perry Mason* was not Raymond Burr. Nor was he their second choice. Fred MacMurray, Robert Sterling, and Efram Zimbalist, Jr., were the leading choices. Burr auditioned for the role of prosecuting attorney Hamilton Burger instead. When writer Erle Stanley Gardner saw Burr's screen test, however, he leaped out of his seat and shouted, "That's Perry Mason!"

❧

"No."

—Doris Day, at a 1957 party, when director Joshua Logan asked her to sing a tune. Logan had wanted to cast Day in the movie version of Rodgers and Hammerstein's *South Pacific*. When she declined his request at the party, he changed his mind about offering the part to her, and she filmed *The Tunnel of Love* instead.

❧

"A goddamn cheap shit voice."

—Actor Rossano Brazzi, star of 1958's movie musical *South Pacific*, of opera singer Giorgio Tozzi. Brazzi couldn't carry a tune and was forced to lip synch to the singing voice of Tozzi, which he found difficult because he thought Tozzi had even less talent than himself.

❦

"We have to stop the show. What are we going to do with a big clunker kid like that?"

—Joe Connelly, producer of *Leave it to Beaver*, when Jerry "the Beav" Mathers turned twelve years old. The show came to an abrupt end, leaving Ward and June frozen in time with a big, clunker kid.

❦

"Please don't do that again."

—Excerpt from 35,000 different letters to the TV producers of Perry Mason, after seeing the episode entitled "The Case of the Deadly Verdict," wherein Perry Mason lost his case. In a later episode, the writers had Mason find the real culprit, so the guilty verdict was overturned.

"This picture stinks. I won't do it for anything."

—Elizabeth Taylor in 1960, to her agent and friends. She didn't want to film *Butterfield 8* but was forced to do it by her contractual agreement with MGM. The film would provide the actress with her only Academy Award. Some say Taylor won the Oscar for this film because she should have won it for *Cat on a Hot Tin Roof* the year before. Others think Liz drew a massive sympathy vote because she'd recently had a tracheotomy. "Hell, *I* even voted for her," confessed Debbie Reynolds, whose husband Eddie Fisher had left her for Taylor.

∽

"If you go into a restaurant and you have to tell them who you are . . . you're not famous."

—Gregory Peck

∽

"Go into your daddies' wallets and remove those little green pieces of paper with pictures of George Washington, Benjamin Franklin, Lincoln, and Jefferson on them. Send them to me, and I'll send you a postcard from Puerto Rico."

—Soupy Sales on January 1, 1965, to his kiddie-show viewers on WNEW-TV, New York City. After receiving a deluge of cash in the mail, the station suspended Sales. He was later reinstated.

༒

James Franciscus and William Shatner were both offered the lead role in the TV series *Dr. Kildare* but turned it down. Producers went with an unknown named Richard Chamberlain, and the role made him a star.

༒

When *The Sound of Music* was released in Seoul, South Korea, one theater manager decided the film was too long, so he shortened it by editing out all of the songs.

༒

"I don't feel we did wrong in taking this great country away from them. There were great numbers of people who needed a new land, and the Indians were selfishly trying to keep it for themselves."

—Actor John Wayne, commenting on Native Americans in the late 1960s

"You know what else is disappearing from the supermarkets' shelves? Toilet paper. There's an acute shortage of toilet paper in the United States."

—This joke from Johnny Carson's December 19, 1973, *Tonight Show* monologue prompted an actual shortage of toilet paper in the United States, as Americans plunged into a three-week toilet paper–buying frenzy.

"Why don't you get your nose fixed?"

—Barbara Walters in the late 1970s to Barbra Streisand, in her first ABC prime-time TV interview program. Some Babs have no qualms about plastic surgery.

> "Nothing will ever separate us. . . . We'll
> probably be married another ten years."

—Elizabeth Taylor in the Chicago *Daily News*, June 21, 1974, about her marriage to Richard Burton. Five days later, she announced that she had filed for divorce.

∾

> "If you go on the air with that crap, they're
> going to kill you dead in the streets!"

—Actor Mickey Rooney to TV producer Norman Lear in 1970, turning down the starring role in a new TV series called *All in the Family*, thinking it would be far too rough for TV audiences to handle. Carroll O'Connor was cast as Archie Bunker instead, and *All in the Family* spent eleven years on the air, half of them as the number one rated TV series.

∾

Talk show host Arsenio Hall saw Rupert Murdoch waiting for his car at the Ivy Restaurant in Los Angeles. Hall went up to introduce himself, and Murdoch handed him his valet parking ticket.

"No, Mr. Murdoch," Hall replied, "I do your show."

"Owl Stretching Time"
"Toad Elevating Moment"
"Sex and Violence"
"A Horse, A Spoon and a Basin"
"Unlike a Bloody Stumbling Boot"
"Gwen Dibley's Flying Circus"

—Original series names considered for what became *Monty Python's Flying Circus*

∽

"Carrie!"

—Mark Hamill in the 1977 George Lucas movie *Star Wars*. Luke Skywalker was supposed to shout "Leia!" after Luke destroys the Death Star and is getting out of his fighter. Instead, he shouted Carrie Fisher's real name. The scene was very complicated and involved many extras, so the director chose not to reshoot it.

∽

"Boulder! John Boulder!"

—Actor Peter Lawford on a TV quiz show, when asked to name a famous singer named John whose last name was a city in Colorado

"A nightmare."

—Actress Sigourney Weaver about the grueling 1979 movie production *Alien*. She swore she'd never do another, but changed her mind and made five.

❧

"You'd all be speaking German if it weren't for us."

—American actor Vince Vaughn, to a crowd of French fans at the Cannes Film Festival, after his hotel accidentally hung the American flag upside down

❧

"Are we going to visit her? I've always liked Betty."

—Peter Lawford to his friend, not understanding that he was being escorted to the Betty Ford drug treatment center, and not on a social call

❧

"87, 79, 78, 70, 69."

—Comedian Tim Allen, when a policeman who stopped him for speeding asked him to count backwards from eighty-seven, for a sobriety test. Allen pleaded not guilty.

∽

"That's a face you'll never see on a lunchbox."

—NBC programming whiz Brandon Tartikoff, after Michael J. Fox replaced first-choice Matthew Broderick for the role of Alex in a new 1982 series called *Family Ties*. But NBC went with Fox anyway, and the show was a major success. Fox became a huge teenage heartthrob, and did eventually turn up on a lunchbox for the movie *Back to the Future* in 1989.

∽

"George Clooney's greatest asset is his ass. We noticed it first on *The Facts of Life*."

—Warren Littlefield, president of NBC Entertainment, in 1987

∽

"I'm Barbara Stanwyck in *The Big Valley*."

—Actress Kim Basinger in 1989, after she purchased the town of Braselton, Georgia, for $20 million. Unlike Stanwyck's TV character, successful rancher Victoria Barkley, Basinger went bankrupt within four years, and she was forced to sell the town.

∽

"This is the best movie we've ever made."

—Mark Canton, head of Warner Bros., in 1990, upon completion of *The Bonfire of the Vanities*. He thought the film would win several Oscars. It was an abysmal failure.

∽

"He's the least weird man I've ever known."

—Elizabeth Taylor defending her friend Michael Jackson in 1991, after he'd suggested Liz use his three giraffes as bridesmaids at her wedding to Larry Fortensky

∽

"And the Oscar goes to . . . genuine cubic zirconia!"

—During Swifty Lazar's 1991 Oscars party, many celebrities were gathered at Spago to watch the Academy Awards show on television. Upstairs, in one of Spago's offices, a waitress decided she'd rather watch the Home Shopping Network. So she changed the channel in the office, unaware that her TV set controlled the 14 monitors in the restaurant. James Stewart, Maggie Smith, Madonna, Ben Kingsley, and Michael Jackson were among those treated to the on-air shopping commentary of people who were not movie fans.

ॐ

"Beyond its entertainment value, *Baywatch* has enriched and, in many cases, helped save lives."

—*Baywatch* star David Hasselhoff, commending the value of the show's lifeguarding techniques

ॐ

"New Jersey?"

—Actress Tori Spelling, when asked to name the capital of New York

"I think stoner dropouts should be writing reviews because they're the most accurate."

—Actress Winona Ryder, who has received mostly positive reviews throughout her career

❧

"I don't like to take my clothes off."

—Actress Demi Moore, shortly before she posed nude for the cover of *Vanity Fair*—twice—and appeared topless in no less than six movies, including *Striptease*

❧

"I'm sincere. I'm really curious. I care what people think. I listen to answers and leave my ego at the door. I don't use the word *I*."

—Talk show host Larry King, in a *Psychology Today* interview

❧

"I was being a good Samaritan."

—Comedian Eddie Murphy, after being caught picking up a transvestite prostitute in L.A.

ॐ

"Anthony Hopkins is here with his wife, who looks like a thin Barbara Bush. Nice to see they've been married for a long time, and they're very happy, from what I hear."

—E! TV hostess Joan Rivers at the 1995 Academy Awards. Hopkins and his wife, Jenni, have been married for many years, but the woman with Hopkins at the Oscars was not his wife, but his mother.

ॐ

"It tastes good, and I think Jenna liked it."

—Actor Matthew McConaughey, about chewing tobacco in between his *EdTV* love scenes with Jenna Elfman

ॐ

"I'm king of the world!"

—Film director James Cameron, after winning the 1998 Academy Award for *Titanic*. Movie buffs recorded more than 200 inconsistencies in the popular film: Rose's eyes change from green to blue, for example, and skates are visible on actors' feet as they slide down sloping corridors.

⤬

"Good-looking people turn me off. Myself included."

—Actor Patrick Swayze

Technology

Great errors made by great people. Perhaps the smarter you are, the harder you err.

"Man will not fly for fifty years."

—Wilbur Wright to his brother, Orville, in 1901. They both flew less than two years later.

༄

"The phonograph . . . is not of any commercial value."

—Thomas Edison, inventor of the phonograph, in 1880. Edison also underestimated the future of moving pictures and electric lights.

"The radio craze . . . will die out in time."

—Thomas Edison in 1922. Guess he could not foresee Wolfman Jack, Dr. Laura, and Howard Stern.

✑

"There is not the slightest indication that [nuclear] energy will ever be obtainable. It would mean that the atom would have to be shattered at will."

—German physicist and Nobel laureate Albert Einstein in 1932. Within seven years, Einstein himself proved that atoms could be shattered and, much to his horror, nuclear energy was obtained for purposes of war.

✑

"Nuclear-powered vacuum cleaners will probably be a reality within ten years."

—Alex Lewyt, president of the Lewyt vacuum cleaner company, in *The New York Times*, June 10, 1955

✑

"They will diminish neuroses and inhibitions, and consequently lead to a decline in the violence of society."

—Eldridge Cleaver, former Minister of Information of the Black Panther Party, who designed a line of men's slacks with a pouch in front for the wearer's sexual organ. The pants were called Cleavers.

℘

"Normal construction problems. . . . You can't use glass without occasionally having some of it break."

—John Hancock insurance executive Albert Prouty, downplaying public concerns about the company's new I. M. Pei–designed Boston skyscraper. Hundreds of windows had started to blow out on a windy night in 1973, starting a regular flow of broken glass to the streets below, which had to be closed. Before long, the first 33 floors of the building were covered in plywood and all 10,340 windows in the new building had to be replaced.

℘

"I would not call it an accident. I would call it a malfunction. . . . It just so happens that the anti-nuclear movement, lacking a real accident, has latched onto this one, promoting it into something that it isn't."

—Dr. Edward Teller, "Father of the hydrogen bomb," in an interview after the Three Mile Island power plant leaked 250,000 gallons of radioactive waste in March 1979

❧

"It looks as though it was put in by an Indian."

—Prince Philip, Duke of Edinburgh, during a factory tour, commenting on a fuse box that looked a little out of place in the state-of-the-art facility. Buckingham Palace later apologized for the remark.

❧

"It can't be something that simple that could cause this to happen."

—Lockheed-Martin vice president Noel Hinners in September 1999, after a $125 million spacecraft known as the Mars Climate Orbiter was lost only 60 miles from its destination. Engineers from NASA and Jet Propulsion Laboratories had incorrectly used metric measurements for the craft's thruster force. That same year, NASA's $203 million Mars Polar Lander also failed. A typo in the software code led the craft to think it had landed when it was still 131 feet off the ground. The probe shut off its engines and crashed. Hey, this *is* rocket science.

War

What it is good for!

"Why, they couldn't hit an elephant with . . ."

—Union General John Sedgwick about a Civil War Confederate assault, in a statement he was unable to complete because he was struck by a bullet

"The United States will not be a threat to us for decades—not in 1945, but at the earliest 1970 or 1980."

—Adolf Hitler to Russian President Vyacheslav Molotov, November 12, 1940

During World War I, Germany wanted to keep the United States from joining in support of Britain, which was languishing and broke. Germany's Foreign Minister, Arthur Zimmerman, decided to recruit Mexico and Japan on his side, just in case the Americans joined in. In return for their help, Zimmerman thought he would offer Mexico the chance to regain Texas, New Mexico, and Arizona. He decided to communicate this idea to the president of Mexico in a telegraph cable, sent in code through Great Britain and the United States. This was his mistake. Unbeknownst to Zimmerman, the Brits had broken the German code, which they shared with the United States. Using this telegram, President Wilson got Congress to declare war against Germany in 1917. Zimmerman was demoted, and Germany lost the war within eighteen months.

❧

"Oh dear, who was she?"

—Actress Joan Crawford in 1941, when told that the Japanese had destroyed Pearl Harbor

❧

"It is not a policy of the North Vietnamese to torture prisoners."

—Jane Fonda, during a period when John McCain was in a prison camp, getting his arms broken for refusing to pose for photos with her

∽

"We are not about to send American boys nine or ten thousand miles away from home to do what Asian boys ought to be doing for themselves."

—President Lyndon B. Johnson during his re-election campaign, October 21, 1964, when there were approximately 20,000 American soldiers in South Vietnam. Within Johnson's next term, the number of American troops there ballooned to more than 500,000.

∽

"If I'd have made the army, we wouldn't have had all that trouble in Vietnam, cuz I would have won it in a year."

—Musician Ted Nugent, on his Detroit radio show in 1996

"U.S. forces dropped sarin, a nerve gas, in Laos in 1970, which killed about a hundred people."

—CNN reporter Peter Arnett, June 7, 1998, in a story repeated in *Time* magazine. This was a scoop that meant that the United States committed a serious war crime during Vietnam. Reporters called it Operation Tailwind. Critics and witnesses denounced the story, and it was learned that the primary evidence was testimony from an 87-year-old retired admiral living in a nursing home who had recently "recovered" such a memory. CNN and *Time* apologized to their audiences, and the producers of the segment were axed. The Joint Chiefs of Staff and the Secretary of Defense released detailed evidence that the report was untrue. The 87-year-old admiral said he was asked "trick questions," and that no gas was ever used.

Current Events

A potpourri of mangled missives and miscalculations.

On July 4, 1848, there was a zinc-lined time capsule placed inside the new foundation for the Washington Monument. However, no one thought to record exactly where the time capsule is, and it has never been located.

෴

"ALL SAVED FROM *TITANIC* AFTER COLLISION; Rescue by *Carpathia* and *Parisian*; Liner is Being Towed to Halifax after Smashing into an Iceberg."

—April 13, 1912, headline in the *Baltimore Evening Sun* and the *New York Sun*, after reporters there misinterpreted several radio messages. The *Los Angeles Express* went on to pick up this story.

"The gravity of the damage to the *Titanic* is apparent, but the important point is that she did not sink."

—*The Wall Street Journal,* quickly congratulating the builders of the *Titanic* for making her truly unsinkable

❧

"No Congress of the United States ever assembled, on surveying the state of the Union, has met with a more pleasing prospect than that which appears at the present time. . . . The country can regard the present with satisfaction and anticipate the future with optimism."

—President Calvin Coolidge, December 4, 1928. Within eleven months, the stock market crash would precede the longest economic depression in American history.

❧

"Any report of a famine in Russia today is an exaggeration or malignant propaganda."

—*New York Times* reporter Walter Duranty in 1933, when Stalin had the Ukraine in the grip of a massive famine to break their resistance to Soviet control

❧

"Baloney. . . . No coalition of racketeers dominates organized crime across the nation."

—J. Edgar Hoover in 1962, when confronted with a huge amount of evidence that the Mafia existed in the United States, including his own surveillance of mobster Sam Giancana with a friend of the president's, Judith Campbell

❧

"My wife is delighted to get away, and it's fun for the kids."

—Former Atomic Energy Commissioner James Schlesinger in 1972, when he took his family on vacation to view nuclear bomb tests on Amchitka Island

"I don't need bodyguards."

—Jimmy Hoffa, Teamsters president, one month before he was abducted in July 1975, never to be seen again

❧

"GUILTY!"

—1995 headline at Time-Warner's online news website, Pathfinder, announcing the O.J. Simpson criminal trial verdict. In a modern-day twist on the old "Dewey Defeats Truman" headline, a Pathfinder spokesman explained: "We had two headlines prepared—one for guilty and one for not guilty—and put the wrong one up."

❧

"It's a good way to get rid of a few nuts, you know. You gotta look at it that way."

—Television impresario Ted Turner, about the 1997 Heaven's Gate cult suicide

❧

**"I was asked to come to Chicago because
Chicago is one of our fifty-two states."**

—Actress Raquel Welch on *Larry King Live*, explaining her appearance at a pro-choice rally

⌇

**"I would have never owned those ugly-ass
shoes."**

—Defendant O.J. Simpson, in a February 1996 civil lawsuit deposition, denying he owned a pair of Bruno Magli "Lorenzo" style shoes, as worn by the murderer of Nicole Simpson and Ron Goldman. One month later, thirty photographs were discovered clearly showing Simpson wearing the same ugly-ass shoes at a 1993 Buffalo Bills game.

⌇

**"Don't stay here too long or you'll get slitty
eyes."**

—Prince Philip in 1996, to a group of British students in China

⌇

"It could have been spinach dip or something."

—Monica Lewinsky, in her 1998 grand jury testimony regarding the stain on her blue dress

Local Issues

Interesting news collected from around the world.

"Morality of city employees is at an all-time low."

—Councilman Jasper Weese of Traverse City, Michigan, during a 1997 commission meeting. Perhaps morale was high, however.

❧

"It's not a cigarette. It's a joint."

—One Barry Shoemaker in 1998, when told by the city manager that cigarette smoking was not allowed during the city council meeting in Harlinden, Texas

"A defense attorney's job is to get his client off, not necessarily to find the truth. It's not a gentile profession."

—The Greenwood (Mississippi) *Commonwealth*

∽

"A young girl who was blown out to sea on a pair of inflatable teeth was rescued—by a man on an inflatable lobster. Two lifeboats had been launched to go to the aid of the child off Boxhull, East Sussex. 'This sort of thing is all too common,' a coastguard spokesman said."

—*The Times* (London). Perhaps the coast guard should trade in their lifeboats for a rescue fleet of inflatable lobsters.

∽

"I thought it was dead."

—Owen Rutherford, an attendant at the Chicago Zoo, after noticing one of his newly arrived Black Mambas wasn't moving. The snake was a new acquisition from Philadelphia, and the attendant suspected it had not survived the move. That is, until he poked it with his finger. Rutherford later recovered from his bite injuries in a Chicago hospital.

"An article on May 7 about the Central Asian lands whose names end in 'stan' referred incorrectly to Kafiristan. It is the former name of a region in northeastern Afghanistan, not an imaginary place invented by Rudyard Kipling."

—*The New York Times*

∽

"Women are best suited for secretarial work, decorating cakes, and counter sales, like selling lingerie."

—South Carolina state representative Larry Koon (R-Lexington)

∽

A man who was fishing in the Amazon got his line stuck in a tree. While disentangling the line, he disturbed a large bees' nest. He was attacked repeatedly by the vicious bees, until he desperately jumped into the water. Unfortunately, once in the water, he was quickly devoured by piranhas.

∽

"The last thing you want is for somebody to commit suicide before executing them."

—Utah director of corrections Gary Deland, about a special holding cell for death row prisoners awaiting execution

❧

"Meanwhile, Richard Parker Bowles, brother of Camilla's ex-husband, Andrew, said that from the beginning, Camilla approved of Charles's marrying Diana while she remained his power mower."

—Richmond Times-Dispatch

❧

"I didn't say I wanted head. I said I wanted to get inside her head."

—Baltimore TV reporter Harry Trout, caught with a prostitute and arrested, claiming he was trying to interview her for a news story. He was acquitted of the charges.

❧

"The following corrects errors in the July 17 geographical agent and broker listing:

United States: Charlotte appeared twice in the North Carolina listing.

International: Aberdeen is in Scotland, not Saudi Arabia or England; Antwerp is in Belgium, not Barbados; Baie Mahault is in Guam, not Guadaloupe; Belfast is in Northern Ireland, not Nigeria; Bogota was listed twice in Colombia; Cardiff is in Wales, not Vietnam; Edinburgh is in Scotland, not England; Helsinki is in Finland, not Fiji; Moscow is in Russia, not Qatar; Nilsen Brothers has an office in Norway, not Oman."

—*Business Insurance* magazine

Politics

Public service inspires many people to speak a different kind of truth.

"I have never heard of anything, and I cannot conceive of anything more ridiculous, more absurd, and more affrontive to all sober judgment than the cry that we are profiting by the acquisition of New Mexico and California. I hold that they are not worth a dollar."

—U.S. Senator Daniel Webster of Massachusetts in 1848

∽

"The Army is the Indian's best friend."

—Gen. George Armstrong Custer in 1870, a few years before his army wiped out most of the Sioux nation at the Little Big Horn River

∽

"Friends, tonight my little wife will be going to sleep in a cramped hotel room on the other side of town, but come next March she'll be sleeping in the White House!"

—William Jennings Bryan, during his unsuccessful 1900 presidential campaign against William McKinley. A religious fanatic, Bryan ran unsuccessfully for president several times. After this proclamation, Bryan waited for cheers from the audience. Instead, a single voice shouted back: "Well, if she does, she'll be sleeping with McKinley, because he's gonna win!"

∽

In the 1962 election, nearly 50,000 voters in Connecticut wrote in Edward M. Kennedy as their choice for United States Senate. Kennedy was not running in Connecticut, however, but in Massachusetts, where he won the seat.

In the 1970s, the town of Picoaza, Ecuador, held a pre-election campaign for the mayor's office. The two candidates were unremarkable. During this same period, a foot powder company called Pulvapies launched a local ad campaign that advised, "Vote for any candidate, but if you want well-being and hygiene, vote for Pulvapies." A few weeks later, the voters in the town of 4,000 elected Pulvapies foot powder to be the mayor of Picoaza.

~

"That's something nobody has to worry about."

—Actor Clint Eastwood in a 1985 *Rolling Stone* interview, when asked if he would ever run for public office. Within a year, he ran for mayor of Carmel, California, and won.

~

"This was not a junket, in any sense of the word."

—U.S. Senator Strom Thurmond, in 1987, after he spent taxpayers' money to take his wife, children, neighbor, and forty friends and staff members on a five-day trip to the Paris Air Show.

~

"Everybody who's for abortion was at one time themselves a feces."

—W.R. Grace chairman Peter Grace, appearing with Ronald Reagan at an anti-abortion rally in New York City

☙

"I will not tolerate intolerance."

—U.S. Senator Bob Dole about Pat Buchanan, during their 1996 rivalry for the Republican presidential nomination

☙

During his 1996 campaign, Louisiana Republican candidate David Duke explained that there had been recent air crashes at TWA and Valuejet "because of affirmative action programs."

☙

"You can get elected by proclaiming that you are
a sodomite and engage in anal sex all the time.
You will get elected."

—U.S. Representative Robert Dornan (R-California), a conservative who was not re-elected for his own seat in 1996

∽

"I did not have sexual relations with that
woman, Monica Lewinsky."

—President Bill Clinton, January 26, 1998

∽

"I believe if I set my mind to it, within the next
fifteen years, I could be president of the United
States."

—Entertainer Will Smith, promoting his popular film *Independence Day*. Thirteen years and counting.

Stupid User Support

Actual customer service encounters from computer companies.

CUSTOMER: Hello, one of my friends gave me an Image Writer printer and this keyboard. He said he gave me all the cables, but I can't figure out how to connect them. Am I missing something?

TECH SUPPORT: Well, a computer would help.

CUSTOMER: You mean this keyboard isn't a word processor?

TECH SUPPORT: No, ma'am, it's just an input device.

CUSTOMER: Then I need to buy a computer, right?

TECH SUPPORT: Yes.

CUSTOMER: Do you think I'll need a monitor too?

CUSTOMER: Excuse me, but my keyboard doesn't work when I take it on business trips.

&

CUSTOMER: Yes, I ordered top of the line components—the best monitor, the best keyboard, printer, speakers, scanner, you name it. But now that it's all here together, I can't get any of them to work.
TECH SUPPORT: Did you order a hard drive?
CUSTOMER: Did I need to order one of those?

&

"I want an Internet. Can I have one of these?"

—Mel B., "Scary" of the Spice Girls, when she saw a computer monitor at an American Online press conference

Music

They may be able to hit all the right notes, but not al-ways the right words.

"I'd rather be dead than singing 'Satisfaction' when I'm forty-five."

—Mick Jagger of the Rolling Stones in a 1970s interview. Now 57, Jagger is alive and well, and just finished a three-year world tour, during which he sang "Satisfaction" numerous times.

❧

"The chimpanzees were scared to death. They scampered all over the place, seeking the protection of their keepers and hiding under benches. . . . One chimp tried to pull the trombone away from Tommy Dorsey."

—A zookeeper at the Philadelphia Zoo in 1949, after Tommy Dorsey and his orchestra gave a concert in the monkey house

❦

"It will be gone by June."

—*Variety* in 1955, about rock and roll music. Perhaps they meant June of the year 2942.

❦

"Disgusting. . . . Thank heaven it is on the way out."

—Dean Martin in the mid 1950s, about rock and roll music. His opinion was shared by Frank Sinatra, who called rock and roll "brutal, ugly, and desperate."

❦

"I thought my new group would take right off."

—Guitarist David Marks, who left the Beach Boys in 1964 to start a new band, Dave and the Marksmen

✑

"We don't think they'll do anything in this market."

—Capitol Records president Alan Livingston in 1964, about an unknown British band called the Beatles, who were about to start their first American tour. Capitol had signed on as the band's American record distributor, but Livingston had modest expectations.

✑

"You know what they say about the Japanese is right! They do all look alike."

—John Lennon, after the Beatles' first tour to the Far East. Lennon had a change of view when he later met Yoko Ono, who was decidedly unique to him, and became his wife.

✑

"If I was a Jewish girl in Hitler's day, I would become his girlfriend. After ten days in bed, he would come to my way of thinking."

—Yoko Ono, exhibiting how she set herself apart

∽

"I never use a baton. But I decided to use one for this performance because I thought it would help achieve greater musical control."

—Uruguayan conductor Jose Serebrier after a 1975 concert in Mexico City, during which he had accidentally stabbed himself through the hand with his baton. Blood gushed from his impaled hand throughout the performance, startling the musicians, but Serebrier continued conducting without missing a beat. During a lull in the music, he removed the wooden baton from the wound, and wrapped his bleeding hand with a handkerchief to finish the show.

∽

"I don't know anything about music. In my line, you don't have to."

—Elvis Presley

"Every chance I get."

—Musician John Denver, when asked if he ever smoked hash. His casual remark became headline news, and Denver had to do some serious backpedaling.

❧

"He has no voice at all—he cannot sing."

—The teacher of Enrico Caruso, one of the greatest opera singers of the 20th century. Caruso also defied his parents, who wanted him to be an engineer.

❧

"We can fly, you know. We just don't think the right thoughts to levitate ourselves off the ground."

—Michael Jackson

❧

"Because I'm an American Indian."

—Entertainer Wayne Newton, when asked why he thought he was invited to a White House state dinner for India's Prime Minister, Indira Gandhi

ॐ

"That's not the kind of artist that I am, luckily. Otherwise I'd never be taken seriously."

—Singer Sinead O'Connor, when asked if she'd ever like to have a number one record. She prefers people take her seriously when she announces she's retired, a Buddhist, a Pope-hater, and a priest.

ॐ

"President Kennedy, as usual, I love you."

—Singer Carly Simon in 1996, at a campaign rally for President Clinton

ॐ

"Who is the loneliest monk?"

—MTV reporter Tabitha Sorenson in 1992, to presidential candidate Bill Clinton, after he said he once dreamed of playing saxophone with Thelonius Monk

❧

"I can't think of a better way to spread the message of world peace than by working with the NFL and being part of Super Bowl XXVII."

—Entertainer Michael Jackson in 1993. Let there be peace on earth, and let it begin with the Cowboys vs. the Bills.

❧

"If women didn't like criminals, there would be no crime."

—Entertainer Ice-T

❧

"I get to go to lots of overseas places, like
Canada."

—Singer Britney Spears. Lake Ponchartrain is a very big lake, after all.

∽

"I resign in Florida."

—14-year-old Floridian and Backstreet Boys singer Nick Carter, in
an interview during which he alarmed his audience, who understood
him to mean that he was leaving the band

∽

"The music of you and your brothers has been
an inspiration to millions."

—U.S. Senator Edward M. Kennedy, mistaking KABC Los Angeles
radio host Michael Jackson with the singer Michael Jackson, which is
very difficult to do even in a telephone interview

Health and Science

Revelations that have helped ordinary people, through the ages.

"On October 13 of this year, there will be a flood as great as Noah's."

—British theologian and mathematician William Whitson in 1736, in what was perhaps the first recorded weather forecast that proved incorrect

ॐ

"The cause of baldness in men is dryness of the brain, and its shrinking from the skull."

—Samuel Johnson, the writer known as "Dr. Johnson," in the late 1700s

"Sensible and responsible women do not want to vote. The relative positions to be assumed by man and woman in the working out of our civilization were assigned long ago by a higher intelligence than ours."

—Former U.S. president Grover Cleveland, 1905

✑

"If [a woman] . . . is normally developed and well-bred, her sexual desire is small. If this were not so, the whole world would become a brothel and marriage and a family impossible."

—Joseph G. Richardson, M.D., et al., professors at the University of Pennsylvania, 1909

✑

"Direct thought is not an attribute of femininity. In this woman is now centuries . . . behind man."

—Thomas A. Edison, in an October 1912 *Good Housekeeping* article called "The Woman of the Future"

"The conjunction of six planets on December 17 could generate a magnetic current that might cause the sun to explode and engulf the earth."

—Meteorologist Albert Porta in 1919

❧

"Mentally slow, unsociable, and adrift forever in his foolish dreams."

—Albert Einstein's elementary school teacher, about her young student, who didn't learn to read until he was seven years old

❧

"Sometime between April 16 and 23, 1957, Armageddon will sweep the world! Millions of persons will perish in its flames and the land will be scorched."

—California pastor Mihran Ask, quoted in *The Watchtower* magazine, distributed by the Jehovah's Witnesses

❧

"The world will end in the fall of 1982."

—Pat Robertson in the 1970s

⌘

"I am so healthy that I expect to live on and on."

—*Prevention* magazine publisher J. I. Rodale on ABC-TV's *Dick Cavett Show* in 1971, minutes before he had a heart attack and died on the air

⌘

In 1972, the Oregon Health Department discovered that the chunks in Hoody Chunky Style Peanut Butter were not peanuts, but rat droppings. Hoody company executives were sentenced to ten days in prison for health violations, and the U.S. Food and Drug Administration issued strict new guidelines on the amount of foreign matter permissible in packaged foods. They include:

1. No more than 50 insect fragments or two rodent hairs per 100 grams of peanut butter
2. No more than ten fruit fly eggs in 100 grams of tomato juice
3. No more than 150 insect fragments in an eight-ounce chocolate bar

"Kahoutek will be the comet of the century."

—Harvard astronomer Fred Whipple in January 1974, along with dozens of other prominent astronomers, who declared that Kahoutek had a tail 50 million miles long. They announced that this enormous comet would stretch across one sixth of the heavens and glow five times brighter than the moon. The excited public spent weeks buying telescopes, binoculars, and T-shirts. But when it finally came, the comet was so tiny that it was barely visible to those with high powered lenses, let alone the naked eye.

∽

In 1975, the Cystic Fibrosis Foundation named six-year-old Rodney Brown of Indiana to be their poster child, as he'd been treated for the disease since the age of one. In 1980, Brown was tested and it was found that he did not have cystic fibrosis after all, and never did.

∽

"There's a high rate of cancer among my friends. It doesn't mean anything."

—Dr. Francis Clifford, Health Commissioner of Niagara County, New York, in the spring of 1978, when asked about the high incidence of cancer among residents who lived next to Love Canal. It was soon learned that the Hooker Chemical Company had been using Love Canal as a toxic waste dump for years, and the neighborhood was permanently evacuated. With all the people gone, cancer rates receded.

❦

"If you eat bananas, your skin will exude an odor which is very attractive to mosquitoes."

—Free advice in a brochure from the Canadian National Park Service, which neglects to mention that maple syrup (plentiful in Canada!) has the same effect

❦

"All the waste in a year from a nuclear power plant can be stored under a desk."

—Ronald Reagan, February 15, 1980, during his presidential campaign. Well, maybe his desk. The average waste in a year is 30 tons of radioactive waste per power plant.

"No one knows more about this mountain than Harry, and it don't dare blow up on him."

—84-year-old Oregon resident Harry Truman on national television in March 1980, pooh-poohing disaster predictions about a nearby volcano, Mt. Saint Helens. The next day, the mountain erupted in an explosion that was 500 times more powerful than the atomic bomb on Hiroshima. Sixty people died, including Harry Truman and his seventeen cats.

◆

"The winter of 1982–83 is going to make last winter seem like moonlight in Miami."

—Newspapers quoting a forecast from MIT meteorologist Hurd C. Willett, in September 1982. The previous winter had been a cold one, but Willett's prediction was off the mark. The winter of 1982–83 was one of the warmest ever.

◆

"Women are less equipped psychologically to 'stay the course' in the brawling arenas of business, commerce, industry, and the professions."

—Republican presidential candidate Pat Buchanan in the early 1990s

❦

"Drinking is the cause of psoriasis."

—Donna Shalala, Secretary of Health and Human Services, who probably meant to say "cirrhosis." But maybe she knows more than we do about skin ailments.

❦

"How do you keep the natives off the booze long enough to get them to pass the test?"

—Prince Philip, to a driving school instructor in Scotland

❦

"The worst drug today is not smack or pot; it's refined sugar. Sugar kills!"

—Actor George Hamilton, who doesn't have to say anything for his perpetual suntan to promote deadly UV exposure and cancerous melanoma

∽

"The trouble with you Egyptians is that you breed too much."

> —Prince Philip, complaining about heavy traffic in Cairo

∽

"The worst thing a man can do is go bald. Never let yourself go bald."

—Businessman and bestselling author Donald Trump, who has never let himself go bald

∽

"If nothing else, the crisis in cosmology demonstrates that there is much more to understanding cosmic history than is immediately revealed in the Big Band theory, however well established it may have become through rigorous testing."

—*The New York Times*

&

"You can't have been here long. You haven't got a pot belly."

—Prince Philip, upon meeting a British tourist in Budapest

Great Field Plays

Also known as the wise world of sports.

Mike Grady, third baseman for the New York Giants in 1899, made a record four errors on one ball.

An easy grounder was hit toward Grady. *Error #1:* Grady bobbled the ball, allowing the batter to reach first base. *Error #2:* Grady tried to catch the runner anyway, and threw to first, but the ball sailed high above the first baseman's glove, allowing the runner to reach second base. *Error #3:* The runner started toward third base while the ball was still being chased. When the first baseman caught the ball, he threw it to Grady to tag the runner out. Grady dropped the ball. *Error #4:* After Grady dropped the ball, the runner passed third base and raced toward home plate. Grady recovered the ball and threw it to the catcher but, once again, he sent it sailing over his head and into the stands. The runner scored. *Official score:* 0 hits, 1 run, 4 errors.

Recovering from a fumble in the 1929 Rose Bowl against Georgia Tech, USC defensive lineman Roy Riegels ran the football 70 yards in the wrong direction. He was stopped at the one-yard line by a teammate, but a quick two-point safety on the next play allowed Georgia Tech to win the game, 8–7. The local fans of 72,000 blamed their loss on "Wrong Way" Riegels, as he was forever known.

$\mathcal{S}$

"Kid, you're too small. You ought to go out and shine shoes."

—Brooklyn Dodgers manager Casey Stengel at a tryout in 1936, to a young hopeful named Phil Rizzuto. Rizzuto signed with the Yankees instead and became a star shortstop. Stengel eventually became Rizzuto's manager, when he joined the Yankees himself in 1949, and they had many successful years on the same team.

$\mathcal{S}$

"I'll eat them up, baby."

—Austrian weightlifter Arnold Schwarzenegger in 1968, declaring he would win the American title from the International Federation of Bodybuilding. He quickly lost to American Frank Zane.

The New York Jets were playing the Oakland Raiders on NBC, November 17, 1968. The Jets had a three-point lead with less than a minute left to play, so NBC felt comfortable enough to switch from the game and begin their scheduled broadcast of the movie *Heidi*. In the final fifty seconds, the Raiders scored two touchdowns and won the game, 43–32, in what soon became known as the "Heidi Bowl." The NBC switchboards were so busy that their entire telephone system broke down.

✍

"We plan absentee ownership. I'll stick to building ships."

—George Steinbrenner in the *New York Times*, January 1973, when asked about his role in the syndicate that had just purchased the New York Yankees from CBS.

✍

"There's a fly ball deep to center field. Winfield is going back, back . . . he hits his head against the wall. It's rolling towards second base!"

—New York Yankee announcer Jerry Coleman

> ### "I hear Carolina's going to start a freshman, and I know you can't win a national championship with a freshman."

—Al McGuire, on the 1981 University of North Carolina basketball team that included a freshman named Michael Jordan. That freshman brought the championship to UNC. Three years later, in the NBA rookie draft, Jordan was passed over by the Houston Rockets (in favor of Hakeem Olajuwon) and the Portland Trail Blazers (for Sam Bowie). While those players were superb picks, neither could rival Jordan's achievement in the sport.

✒

> ### "Our offense is like the Pythagorean theorem: There is no answer."

—L.A. Lakers star Shaquille O'Neal. The analogy is misstated, but three points for the very long attempt!

✒

> ### "I was misquoted."

—Charles Barkley, referring to objectionable parts of *Outrageous*, which was his own autobiography

"Histrionics are against him."

—TV announcer John Tesh during the 1996 Olympic games, about a gymnast's odds to win a medal. History is against Tesh returning as a sports announcer.

∽

"I don't know. I've never played there."

—Masters golf champion Sandy Lyle in the mid 1990s, when he was asked his opinion about Tiger Woods

∽

"I can't really remember the names of the clubs that we went to."

—Shaquille O'Neal, when asked if he visited the Parthenon during his trip to Greece

∽

"They say Elvis is dead. He's not dead. He's just a different color, he's six foot eight inches, 225 pounds, plays basketball, and he's black."

—Dennis Rodman, in *USA Today*

"Who holds the record for the most babes in a single season—Hornsby, Musial, Ruth, or Cobb?"

—Message board for fans at Oakland Coliseum, during an Athletics game. Yes, but which of them ever got past third base?

&

"If there's a pile-up, they'll have to give some of the players artificial insemination."

—TV announcer Curt Gowdy during the rain delay of an all-star football game where the field was flooded

&

"Men, I want you thinking of one word all season. One word and one word only: 'Sugar Bowl.' "

—Florida State football coach Bill Peterson

&

In 1999, Islanders hockey director of personnel Gordie Clark announced at the NHL Entry Draft that his team was selecting Nelson Pyatt as their eighth pick. Nelson Pyatt had retired years earlier. He meant to pick Taylor Pyatt, Nelson's son.

✑

"The word 'genius' isn't applicable in football. A genius is a guy like Norman Einstein."

—Former quarterback Joe Theisman, on ESPN

✑

"I tell you, that Michael Jackson is unbelievable, isn't he? Three plays in twenty seconds!"

—Al Gore, during the 1998 NBA Finals, of Michael Jordan

Genius for the Defense

Actual attorney dialogue, as taken from court transcripts.

Q: "Was that the same nose you broke as a child?"
A: "I only have one, you know."

Here's one defendant who chose to represent himself:

Q: "Did you get a good look at my face when I took your purse?"

He was found guilty.

Q: "And he said what?"
A: "He says, 'I have to kill you because you can identify me.' "
Q: "And did he kill you?"

❧

Q: "So you were gone until you returned?"

❧

Q: "How long have you been a French Canadian?"

❧

Q: "How many times have you committed suicide?"

❧

Q: "Do you have any children, or anything of that kind?"

Q: "You don't know what it was, and you didn't know what it looked like, but can you describe it?"

❧

Q: "Were you acquainted with the deceased before or after he died?"

❧

Q: "What is your relationship to the plaintiff?"
A: "She's my daughter."
Q: "Was she your daughter on February 14, 1990?"

❧

Q: "So, when he woke up the next morning, he was dead?"

Fearless Leaders

Being in charge does not always mean you are in the know.

"The French people are incapable of killing their King."

—King Louis XVI of France in 1789, three years before he was convicted of treason and guillotined by the French people

⁗

The Mayor of St. Pierre, Martinique, in 1902, forbade the town's residents to flee the active volcano, Mt. Pelee, because important elections were taking place. A lethal eruption cloud soon wiped out the town of 30,000 in two minutes.

"The President spent most of his time entering Mrs. Galt."

—A *Washington Post* typo in 1915, after President Woodrow Wilson went to the theater with his fiancée, Edith Galt, but was observed to be entertaining her more than watching the play

❧

"Gaiety is the most outstanding feature of the Soviet Union."

—USSR leader Joseph Stalin in 1935, when the Soviet Union was implementing massive Communist "purges" and executions of dissenters

❧

"Hitler is a queer fellow who will never become Chancellor; the best he can hope for is to head the Postal Department."

—Field Marshal Paul von Hindenburg, president of Germany, 1931

❧

"I believe that Providence has chosen for me a great work."

—Adolf Hitler, September 11, 1932

❧

"For the second time in our history, a British Prime Minister has returned from Germany bringing peace with honor. I believe it is peace for our time. . . . Go home and get a nice quiet sleep."

—Great Britain's prime minister Neville Chamberlain on a September 10, 1938, radio address. It was not peace for their time, but the eve of the Second World War.

❧

"They should resolve their disputes like good Christians."

—Warren Austin, the American ambassador to the United Nations, urging that Arabs and Jews end the Middle East war of 1948

❧

"You know, Don, if I'm elected we'll end this war in six months."

—Republican presidential candidate Richard M. Nixon to Congressman Don Riegle of Michigan in 1968. Nixon was elected, but the war dragged on for seven more years, until after Nixon left office.

✑

"The police were not there to provoke disorder. They were there to maintain disorder."

—Chicago mayor Richard M. Daley, during that city's 1968 riots

✑

"The streets are safe in Philadelphia. It's only the people who make them unsafe."

—Frank Rizzo, former police chief and mayor of Philadelphia

✑

"Don't confuse me with the facts."

—Chicago mayor Richard M. Daley, to a reporter in 1968

"I hope that Spiro Agnew will be completely exonerated and found guilty of the charges against him."

—Texas governor John Connelly in 1972, attempting to defend the vice president shortly before he resigned and pleaded no contest to tax evasion

"There can be no whitewash at the White House."

—President Richard M. Nixon, December 20, 1973

"It will be years—not in my time—before a woman will become prime minister of England."

—Margaret Thatcher, 1974, five years before she became prime minister

"When the president does it, that means it's not illegal."

—President Richard M. Nixon, 1974, offering a legal interpretation later echoed by President Bill Clinton

✀

"Discovering a cure for cancer will only change which way you're going to go."

—U.S. Representative Earl Landgrebe of Indiana, voting against a 1970s bill to appropriate funds for cancer research

✀

"I am not a chauvinist. . . . I believe in women's rights for every woman but my own."

—Chicago mayor Harold Washington

✀

"This is beautiful. I've always wanted to see the Persian Gulf."

—U.S. Senator William Scott of Virginia, in 1975, on a tour of the Suez Canal with Egyptian president Anwar el-Sadat, who didn't have the heart to tell Scott that the Persian Gulf was nearly a thousand miles away

"Here is President Reagan's favorite recipe for crabmeat casserole."

—Excerpt from a 1981 letter from the White House to an Illinois woman who had written to the President about the unemployment crisis

⚬

"There are two kinds of truth. There are real truths, and there are made-up truths."

—Washington, D.C., mayor Marion Barry, upon his arrest for drug use

⚬

"Here's a toast to Prince Charles and his lovely lady, Princess David."

—President Ronald Reagan in 1984, at a White House state dinner for Prince Charles and Princess Diana. Peter Ustinov was heard whispering to another guest, "He must be thinking about next weekend at Camp Diana."

⚬

"What makes him think a middle-aged actor
who's played with a chimp could have a future in
politics?"

—Ronald Reagan, April 1986, after Clint Eastwood was elected
mayor of Carmel, California

∽

"It's wonderful to be here in the great state of
Chicago!"

—Vice President Dan Quayle

∽

"For those who died, their lives will never be
the same."

—U.S. Senator Barbara Boxer, after the 1983 San Francisco
earthquake

∽

"People don't want handouts! People want hand
jobs!"

—Connecticut governor William O'Neil at a political rally

"That's fine, phonetically, but you're missing just
a little bit."

—Vice President Dan Quayle to sixth-grader William Figueroa of
Trenton, New Jersey, as he added an *e* to the boy's spelling of *potato*

&

"You can't just let nature run wild."

—Alaska governor Walter Hickel, endorsing a state slaughter of
wolves

&

"Capital punishment is our society's recognition
of the sanctity of human life."

—U.S. Senator Orrin Hatch (R-Utah)

&

"Wait a minute! I'm not interested in
agriculture. I want the military stuff."

—U.S. Senator William Scott, during a briefing about missile silos

"The Congress will push me to raise taxes, and I'll say no, and they'll push, and I'll say no, and they'll push again. And all I can say to them is Read My Lips: No New Taxes."

—George Bush in 1988, accepting the Republican nomination for president. President Bush raised income taxes in 1991—without any pushing from Congress—and promptly lost his bid for a second term.

&

"U.N. goodwill may be a bottomless pit, but it's by no means limitless."

—Former British prime minister John Major

&

"With these words I want to assure you that I love you, and if you had been a woman I would have considered marrying you, although your head is full of gray hairs, but as you are a man that possibility doesn't arise."

—Ugandan president Idi Amin, in a letter to Tanzanian president Nyerere

"We will not close any military base that is not needed."

—Secretary of Defense Les Aspin

❧

"We have no political prisoners—only Communists, people who disagree with our rule."

—Park Chung Hee, president of South Korea

❧

"That's the way the cookie bounces."

—New Orleans mayor Vic Schiro

❧

"And now, will you all stand and be recognized?"

—Texas statehouse speaker Gib Lewis on Disability Day, acknowledging a group of capitol visitors who were in wheelchairs

"It's a vast right-wing conspiracy that has been conspiring against my husband since the day he announced for president."

—Hillary Rodham Clinton on the *Today* show, January 27, 1998, denying that her husband dallied with White House intern Monica Lewinsky

Mean Cuisine

Mother always told you not to play with your food.

"Please take our dog into the kitchen and find it something to eat."

—A pair of Swiss tourists, in 1971, to the head waiter at a Hong Kong restaurant, as they sat down for dinner. The couple was aghast when, a few minutes later, their beloved dog, Rosa, was served to them in a frying pan under a sweet-and-sour sauce, with vegetables.

"They do it in all the restaurants in America."

—The owner of the very popular Heavenly Moon restaurant in Beijing, when it was learned he served a special oyster sauce containing pure opium paste

"A story in Wednesday's *News Journal* about beach businesses returning to normal did not clearly state that the freezer at Peg Leg Pete's filled with maggots was not in use.
  "The old freezer was being used as a Dumpster behind the building."

—*Pensacola News Journal*

"Peanut butter is a darn good shaving cream."

—Arizona Republican Barry Goldwater

***Beef Tenderloin with Stilton Cheese, Pastry and
Madeira Sauce***
(6 servings)

Stilton-Walnut Butter (recipe follows)

6 slices brioche or firm white bread, ½ to ¾ inch
    thick
3 tablespoons butter, at room temperature
2 pounds baby, stems removed and discarded
Salt and freshly ground black pepper to taste

> —*The Washington Post.* Some may prefer baby with stems.

∾

"The secret of the restaurant's atmosphere lies
in the fact that it is indeed run by a family, who
restored the building, and now cook and serve
the clients themselves."

—St. Petersburg (Russia) *Press*

∾

Actor Mickey Rooney invented a round frankfurter that could fit on a hamburger bun, and called it a Weenie Whirl. He opened several Mickey Rooney's Weenie Whirl restaurants, but the endeavor was a failure. Rooney, it seems, was no weenie whirl when it came to culinary innovation.

Business

"The horse is here to stay, but the automobile is only a novelty, a fad."

—The president of the Michigan Savings Bank in 1903, to Horace Rackham, Henry Ford's lawyer, advising him not to invest in the Ford Motor Company

❧

"They can buy the automobile in any color so long as it's black."

—Henry Ford in 1913, about his new Model T. Ford assumed consumers didn't care about color, and didn't offer any until 1926, when he needed a boost in sales.

"As sure as I am standing here, this Depression will soon pass and we are about to enter a period of prosperity the likes of which no country has ever seen before."

—Walter S. Gilford of AT&T on November 25, 1930. The Depression lasted nearly a decade, a period of recession the likes of which no country had ever seen before.

⤜⤛

"Why, it's the best education in the world for those boys, that traveling around! They get more experience in a few months than they would in years at school."

—Henry Ford, after putting 75,000 men out of work in 1930, forcing them to hit the roads as "hoboes" looking for work

⤜⤛

"I see no reason why 1931 should not be an extremely good year."

—Alfred P. Sloan, Jr., head of General Motors, in January 1931. It turned out to be one of the worst years of the Great Depression.

"Liquidate labor, liquidate stocks, liquidate the farmer, liquidate real estate . . . people will work harder, live a more moral life. Values will be adjusted and enterprising people will pick up the wrecks from less competent people."

—U.S. treasury secretary Andrew Mellon in 1931, advising President Herbert Hoover to do nothing about the Great Depression. Hoover didn't do much of anything, except remove Mellon as his secretary of the treasury.

❧

"It contains 52 fundamental errors."

—Parker Company executives in 1934, unanimously turning down a proposed idea for a board game called "Monopoly." Eventually, Parker changed its mind and introduced the game, which is still selling like crazy many decades later.

❧

In 1938, physicist Chester Carlson invented and named xerography, a process to make paper duplicates of documents. After he patented the idea, he approached more than twenty companies to manufacture and market his invention, including Kodak and IBM, but they all turned him down. In 1947, in Rochester, New York, a floundering business called the Haloid Company agreed to make the machines. The company changed its name and, in 1958, Xerox introduced its first office copier.

∞

In the late 1970s, IBM decided the truly profitable future of personal computers would be manufacturing the hardware, not the programs to run the machines. After all, this was a business *machine* company (never mind that IBM had rejected Chester Carlson's office copying machine a few decades earlier). Rather than using one of the hundreds of in-house software designers, IBM decided to contract out this "less important" component of the business in 1980. They gave the task to a 25-year-old entrepreneur named Bill Gates, who was happy to transform an old DOS system into MS-DOS, named for Microsoft, and license it to IBM. By 1986, at age 31, Gates was a billionaire.

∞

"In my humble opinion, the picture will be a colossal flop. It lacks dazzle, charm, wit, and imagination."

—Business reporter William Flanagan's October 31, 1977, *New York* magazine article about the movie *Close Encounters of the Third Kind*. The stock in Columbia Pictures plummeted immediately, and the New York Stock Exchange halted trading of Columbia stock. Within days, however, reviewers raved about *Close Encounters*, and the movie became Columbia's most profitable film ever.

✌

"De Lorean's dream is selling well."

—*Newsweek* magazine headline in January 1982, about former GM executive John De Lorean's new Belfast car company. De Lorean's dream never sold well, and one month after this headline, the company went bankrupt.

Memorable Advertising Slogans

The 1950s provided a market hungry for new products, and many opportunities for alluring advertisements. These ads ran in Time *and* Life *magazines during a single month, January 1952.*

"I wash 22,000 dishes a year . . . but I'm proud of my pretty hands!" Mrs. Dorian Mehle of Morrisville, Pa., is all three: a housewife, a mother, and a very lovely lady. You and Dorian Mehle have something in common. Every year, you wash a stack of dishes a quarter-mile high!

Yet Dorian hasn't given up detergents. And if she could step off the printed page, you'd find that her hands are as soft, as smooth, as young-looking as a teenager's. Dorian's husband is the best testimonial to Jergens Lotion care. After years of married life, he still loves to hold her hands!

Use Jergens Lotion—avoid detergent hands.

20,679 Physicians say
"Luckies are less irritating. It's toasted."
Your Throat Protection against irritation
and cough

—Lucky Strike cigarettes

❧

When your throat
Calls for a rest
Mild and mellow
KOOLS are best!
THROAT SENSITIVE?
Smoke KOOLS as your steady smoke for that
clean, KOOL taste!

❧

"Not a cough in a carton"

—Old Gold cigarettes

❧

More doctors smoke Camels than any other
cigarette.

❧

Why did you change to Camels, Henry Fonda?
"My voice is important in my career. I smoke
Camels because they're mild and have such rich
flavor!"

Not one single case of throat irritation due to
smoking Camels—that's what noted throat
specialists reported in a coast-to-coast test of
hundreds of people who smoked only Camels
for thirty days!

❧

Filtered cigarette smoke is better for your
health. The nicotine and tars trapped by this
Viceroy filter cannot reach your mouth, throat or
lungs!

❧

When coughs and colds
Have set you choking
A switch to KOOLS
Means tasteful smoking!
GOT A COLD?
Smoke KOOLS as your steady smoke for that
clean, KOOL taste!

⌁

"Man! This is the easiest hard day's work I've
ever done!"
Bless Edison's Televoice!
1 girl serves 20 dictators!
Or more! Forget the secretary shortage—
Televoice cuts instrument dictation costs as
much as 66⅔%.

(And allows 1 girl to paint all her nails!)

⌁

Don't fool with INFECTIOUS DANDRUFF
Start with Listerine Antiseptic . . . Quick!
You simply douse it on the scalp, full strength,
and massage twice a day. It kills millions of
germs associated with infectious dandruff.

(And if it doesn't cure your dandruff, just gargle it to cure bad breath!)

༄

Winter sports to enjoy with Ballantine Ale:
—SKATING at Sun Valley, Idaho
—CURLING at Boston, Massachusetts
—SKIING at The Lodge, Stowe, Vermont

(At least they didn't include DRIVING to granny's house in Dubuque!)

༄

I dreamed I was an eskimo in my Maidenform bra.
Guess whose figure is going around in Arctic
circles?
It's mine and it's marvelous
Here on top of the world we know
What makes the world go round . . . it's
Maidenform.

"Nothing to break the spell."
New Westinghouse Hi-Value TV Gives You
Greatest Eye Comfort Uninterrupted
enjoyment . . . not annoying streaks, flutter,
flopover every time a truck or automobile goes
by, or a plane passes overhead!

～

What makes people fat?
People get fat simply because they overeat
　　Why do they overeat?
Because they're hungry
　　Why are they hungry?
Because their blood sugar level is low
　　What is the fastest way to raise the blood
　　sugar level and help keep from overeating?
Sugar and the good things containing it!
Sugar helps keep your appetite and weight
under control.
Tame your appetite . . . Just eat or drink
something with sugar in it.
Sugar must be one of our most needed foods—
that's why we like it so much.

—The Sugar Information Institute

Another ad for the dieter:

> A Bacardi cocktail has less calories than 2 slices of pineapple!
> Bacardi doesn't taste like whiskey—It doesn't taste like gin
> Try a delicious Bacardi Cocktail—only 88 calories!

✍

> Amazing Asbestos!
> Progressive communities the country over have found their best buy in water mains is "Century" Asbestos-Cement Pipe—moderate in initial cost—it will not rust or corrode—which helps to keep pumping costs low.
> Nature made Asbestos . . . Keasbey & Mattison has made it serve mankind since 1873.

✍

> Revolutionary new hair dressing—*won't grease-stain your hat!*
> Hair experts said it couldn't be done!

✍

Why reeks the goat—on yonder hill,
Who daily dines on chlorophyll?
Don't be the goat

✑

And one more magazine ad, from 1958:

**"The Edsel is a success. It's a new idea—it's a
you idea."**

—Ford Motor Company ad for an automobile already being criti-
cized as a gas-guzzling lemon. More like a through idea.

Now in Theaters

TITLE IN HONG KONG	ENGLISH TITLE
"This Hit Man Is Not as Cold as He Thought"	*The Professional*
"Six Stripped Warriors"	*The Full Monty*
"Mysterious Murder in Snowy Cream"	*Fargo*
"The Big Liar"	*Nixon*
"Don't Ask Me Who I Am"	*The English Patient*
"Mr. Cat Poop"	*As Good As It Gets*

Bibliography

Bacon, James. *How Sweet It Is: The Jackie Gleason Story*. St. Martin's Press, New York, 1985.

Cerf, Christopher, and Victor Navasky. *The Experts Speak*. Pantheon, New York, 1984.

Columbia Journalism Review, Vol. 37, September/October 1998; January/February 1999.

Discover, Vol. 21, April 2000.

Esquire, December 1995.

Felton, Bruce, and Mark Fowler. *The Best, Worst and Most Unusual*. Galahad, New York, 1976.

Goldberg, M. Hirsh. *The Blunder Book*. Quill, New York, 1984.

Hadleigh, Boze. *Hollywood and Whine*. Birch Lane, Secaucus, NJ, 1998.

Kelley, Kitty. *The Royals.* Simon and Schuster, New York, 1997.

Knight-Ridder News Service, March 28, 2000.

Nelson, Craig. *Bad TV.* Delta, New York, 1995.

The New York Times, December 8, December 14, 1999.

The New Yorker, October 30, 1995; January 22, 1996; March 6, 2000.

Newsweek, August 24, 1999.

Stallings, Penny. *Forbidden Channels.* HarperCollins, New York, 1991.

Time, January 7, January 14, January 21, January 28, 1952.

The Wall Street Journal, January 4, 2000.

The Washington Post, June 19, 1987.

Weiner, Ed. *The TV Guide TV Book.* HarperCollins, New York, 1992.

Wiley, Mason, and Damien Bona. *Inside Oscar.* Ballantine, New York, 1986.